WHITE WOLVES

YEAR 3

Stories with Familiar Settings

ANN WEBLEY

Teachers' Resource for Guided Reading

A & C Black • London

Contents

White Wolves Series Consultant: Sue Ellis, Centre for Literacy in Primary Education

First published 2004 by
A & C Black
Bloomsbury Publishing Plc
50 Bedford Square
London
WC1B 3DP

www.acblack.com

Text copyright © 2004 Ann Webley
Illustrations copyright © 2004 Alison Bartlett, Ian Newsham and Michael Reid

The rights of Ann Webley to be identified as the author and the rights of Alison Bartlett, Ian Newsham and Michael Reid to be identified as the illustrators of this work have been asserted by them in accordance with the Copyrights, Designs and Patents Act 1988.

ISBN 978-0-7136-7025-7

A CIP catalogue for this book is available from the British Library.

This book is produced using paper that is made from wood grown in managed, sustainable forests. It is natural, renewable and recyclable. The logging and manufacturing processes conform to the environmental regulations of the country of origin.

Printed and bound in Great Britain by Caligraving Ltd, Norfolk

3 5 7 9 10 8 6 4

Introduction

What is Guided Reading?

Guided Reading is an important aspect of literacy work in the classroom and provides the opportunity for you to reinforce previous teaching from shared sessions. Since the Guided Reading group is small and the children are all of similar ability, teaching can be even more closely targeted in order to ensure understanding and progression.

Aims of Guided Reading

The ultimate aim of Guided Reading at Key Stage 2 is to help the children read independently. This means not only reading accurately and with expression, but being able to read beyond the simple meaning of the words in order to infer, deduce, justify and evaluate. These aspects of reading comprehension need to be taught and, therefore, you play a crucial role in choosing good quality, challenging texts and in guiding sessions at the correct pace.

How to organise Guided Reading

In planning this Guide, it has been assumed that each group has one session of Guided Reading a week. This should take place outside the Literacy Hour to ensure that you can concentrate fully on the group. Other children in the class may be doing a variety of activities depending upon age and/or ability, for example:

- working on an activity based on the previous Guided Reading session.

- reading on independently in order to prepare for discussion in the next session.

- reading a book of their own choice.

- making a personal response in a Reading Journal.

- working with a Teacher Assistant to reinforce work done during a Guided Reading session and to have extra reading practice.

These might be set up in a timetable that the children become very familiar with, thus ensuring an immediate start and full use of time.

Record Keeping

You should briefly fill in notes related to each session in order to inform progression against group and individual targets. A verbatim account is certainly not needed. Instead, it is useful to note children who do not achieve targets or who exceed them in any way. See page 42 for a photocopiable record card template.

Reading Journals

Children could begin to keep a Reading Journal. They can complete any written work based on their Guided Reading book or the Class Book in this journal. As they become used to using it, they should be encouraged to make additional personal responses to what they read: this might be books read at school or at home. Some teachers find it useful to provide children with a list of ideas to get them started. Personal responses ensure that children are engaging with texts and using the strategies they are being taught in Shared and Guided Reading

How to Use This Book

Lessons

This Guide outlines five lessons to support the use of each of the three Year 3 books with a Guided Reading group. The books are:

- *Detective Dan* – for children who need a lot of support with reading.
- *Buffalo Bert, the Cowboy Grandad* – for children who have an average level of reading experience.
- *Treasure at the Boot-fair* – for more experienced readers.

It is important to remember that, although these lessons take into account important elements of reading at Year 3, they cannot be directed at individual children's needs on a specific word or comprehension level. It may, therefore, be necessary to make some adjustments in order to cover the specific reading objectives that a group needs to ensure progress.

Activity Sheets

Activity sheets are included for follow-up work either in school or at home for homework. Children should also be encouraged to write independently in a Reading Journal (see p. 3).

Lesson Duration

The lessons have been planned to be around 20–30 minutes in length but could be amended to suit an individual school's timetables.

Each session should be a mix of reading aloud, reading independently and a discussion about the text. The actual amounts of time spent on each will depend on the independence of the children. Experienced readers should spend most of their time on higher order reading skills, for example prediction, inference and deduction. They may read or re-read certain sections during the session in order to support this work.

Less-experienced readers will need to spend more time each session reading aloud and you will be checking for pronunciation, phrasing and understanding of unfamiliar words. Although there are some suggestions in lesson plans for this part of the session, it is expected that you will make greatest adaptations here because you will need to focus directly on your knowledge of the needs of the group. When helping children over difficulties, you should reinforce the method you are using:

- phonics – the sound of the word.
- graphic – the look of the word.
- semantic – the meaning of the word – can this be guessed by reading on?
- contextual – the context in which the story is set.

In this way, children will get used to using these methods and this will help them towards independence. Other means of developing higher order reading skills will emerge through focussed discussion in other parts of each session.

Target Statements for Reading

The NLS target statements for reading at Year 3 will help you focus on the different elements necessary for progression in reading.

Word recognition and phonic knowledge:
- recognise a range of prefixes and suffixes to construct the meanings of words in context.
- recognise the function of the apostrophe for omission and pronounce contracted forms correctly.
- recognise the full range of consonant digraphs, e.g. kn, wr, ph.

Grammatical awareness:
- read aloud with intonation and expression taking account of punctuation, e.g. commas to mark pauses and grammatical boundaries.
- understand how pronouns in first, second and third person forms are used in sentences and apply this information to maintain understanding when reading.
- understand how dialogue is punctuated and laid out and read with appropriate expression.

Use of context:
- know how language is used to create effects, e.g. adjectives and adverbs for description and use to create detailed mental images.

Interpretations and response: literary text:
- when reading aloud show awareness and understanding of the different voices in stories.
- discuss the actions of the main characters and justify views using evidence from the text.

Attitude:
- sustain silent reading to include longer, more complex texts.
- draw on knowledge of authors and types of books they write to inform choices.
- read aloud confidently to an audience, e.g. favourite passage from a selected text.

Detective Dan – by Vivian French

About the book

This is a mystery story set in the familiar setting of a primary school. Dan and Billy are best friends and do everything together. When Dan has a problem, naturally Billy sets out to help him. Someone is throwing Dan's lunch box on the floor and, eventually, manages to nibble the sandwiches. Dan and Billy turn detective to reveal the culprit – causing mayhem in the classroom in the process. Eventually, they discover who's to blame.

"No," said Dan. "I didn't feel hungry."

"Mrs Harper says Dan is getting *very* untidy," Billy told Mum.

"Yes," Dan said. "And she said that I shouldn't talk to Minnie!"

"Is that the school cat?" Mum asked.

"Yes." Dan frowned. "It's not fair. I don't mean to talk to Minnie, but Minnie always comes to talk to me!"

Dan stamped crossly all the way home again.

On Wednesday afternoon Dan and Billy rushed out of school.

8

9

Detective Dan: Lesson 1

Summary of Chapter One

Dan is very upset as he comes out of school with his friend Billy. On Monday and Tuesday his lunch box is thrown on to the floor. On Wednesday he finds that his sandwiches have been nibbled. The boys tell Dan's mum that Mrs Harper was cross and accused Dan of letting Minnie, the school cat, into the classroom.

Lesson plan

Introduction

Look at the front cover and read the blurb. Ask the children:

- Where will this story be set?
- Who are the main characters in the story?
- What do the children think the story will be about?

Reading

Read the chapter out loud in the group, concentrating at first on accurate reading and expression.

1) If necessary, demonstrate how to read sentences in order to show the sense.

2) Make sure that the children realise that the italics in the chapter help to show how to read aloud. Ask the children how it helps tell the reader about the character's feelings.

3) Check pronunciation of "frowned" and "followed" – same phoneme making a different sound. Focus on any words the children have difficulties with and discuss ways to read them.

Understanding the story

These questions could be asked during reading or at the end of the chapter. Encourage the children to find the appropriate part in the text and not to try to rely on memory.

1) On which days did Dan have problems with his lunch box? (Monday and Tuesday)

2) Why is Dan upset? Encourage the children to explain that it is partly what has happened to his lunch box and partly the reaction of his teacher.

3) Ask the children to find some words which tell us that Dan is upset e.g: "stamped crossly" (p. 6)

4) What did Mrs Harper say? (She said that Dan was untidy and that he shouldn't let the cat in.)

5) Do the children have any idea why Minnie might have followed Dan? (Some children may notice that Dan said someone nibbled his sardine sandwich. They may make a connection with cats liking sardines.)

> **What to do next:** The children can now complete Activity Sheet 1: "Missing sandwiches" which asks some questions based on the chapter.

Missing sandwiches

1. Why was Dan upset?

Dan was upset because _____

_____

_____

_____

2. Why was Mrs. Harper cross with Dan?

Mrs. Harper was cross with Dan because _____

_____

_____

_____

3. Why did Dan want extra big sardine sandwiches for tea?

Dan wanted extra big sardine sandwiches

for tea because _____

_____

_____

Detective Dan: Lesson 2

Summary of Chapter Two

Dan has cheese sandwiches on Thursday. Billy says that he is going to be a detective and find out what is happening to Dan's lunch box. They see Minnie but the cat is not so friendly – another mystery to solve! Billy asks to go to the toilet so that he can look around the cloakroom for clues. Mrs. Harper tells the two boys that they must stay in at playtime because they have been whispering in class. She is very surprised when they seem so pleased. They tell her that Billy is a detective and is going to find out about the lunch box. She tells them to read quietly.

Lesson plan

Introduction

Ask the children to summarise what has happened so far in three sentences.

Reading

Read the chapter out loud in the group, concentrating at first on accurate reading and expression.

1) If necessary, demonstrate how to read sentences in order to show the sense.

2) Focus on any words the children have difficulties with and discuss ways to read them. In particular: silent "k" in "know" (p. 13); "detective" (p. 13) – break the word into syllables to read it; "wriggled" and "struggled" (p. 14); compound words such as "classroom".

Understanding pronouns

Ask one of the children to re-read the third paragraph on p. 12. Make sure the children realise who "you" and "I" refer to. Make sure the children observe the use of pronouns elsewhere in the book.

Understanding the story

Ask the children some of the following questions to check their understanding of the story. Questions could be asked during reading or at the end of the chapter. Encourage the children to find the appropriate part in the text and not to try to rely on memory.

1) Why was Dan happier when he got to school on Thursday?

2) Why do the children think that Minnie is not interested in Dan on Thursday morning?

3) Look at the picture on p. 17. Why were the boys whispering in class? (The children may start to suggest several reasons which would all show understanding of the story: they don't want to get into trouble so they are whispering rather than talking more loudly; they are being detectives so that means being secretive; they are excited about what they are planning and so they are talking even though they shouldn't.)

4) Why were Dan and Billy glad that they could not go out to play? Do the children think Mrs. Harper expected them to be pleased? (The children may start to talk about the fact that being kept in at playtime is usually a punishment.)

> **What to do next:** The children can now complete Activity Sheet 2: "Match the words" which is about reading compound words.

Match the words

A compound word is made from two other words.

Draw lines to match the first word with the second and make the compound word. Some of the words are in the chapter and you will read the others in the next chapter.

 Play   prints

Class   body

 Finger   ground

 Every   time

 Dinner   room

After   noon

White Wolves

Teachers' Resource for Guided Reading Year 3

Stories with familiar settings

© **A & C Black 2004**

Detective Dan: Lesson 3

Summary of Chapter Three

When Mrs Harper leaves the room, the boys decide to check for fingerprints by putting chalk dust on the lunch boxes. This makes the children sneeze when they collect their boxes at dinner time. Mrs Harper is very cross and tells them to stop being detectives. The boys are miserable as they leave school. They tell Dan's mum that no one ate the sandwiches that day but they were kept in at lunchtime. Everyone was cross with them and there was no story at the end of the day.

Lesson plan

Introduction

Ask the children to talk to a partner and tell each other in one minute what has happened in the story so far.

Reading

Read the chapter out loud in the group, concentrating at first on accurate reading and expression.

1) If necessary, demonstrate how to read sentences in order to show the sense.

2) Focus on any words the children have difficulties with and discuss ways to read them. The children should recognise the compound words that they found in the activity sheet.

Understanding the story

Ask the children some of the questions below to check their understanding of the story. Questions could be asked during reading or at the end of the chapter. Encourage the children to find the appropriate part in the text and not to try to rely on memory.

1) Make sure the children know which day of the week it is and what time of day.

2) What was Billy's plan? Ask the children whether they think it was a good one.

3) Look at the picture on pp. 24 and 25. What happened when the children went to collect their lunch boxes at dinnertime? How do the children feel? The children should mention that they also got chalk all over their jumpers (p. 29).

4) Ask the children why they think nothing happened to Dan's lunch box on Thursday. Can they make the link with the different sorts of sandwiches?

What to do next: The children can now complete Activity Sheet 3: "How do they feel" which is about how different characters feel.

How do they feel?

Write inside the speech bubble what you think the characters would say at the end of the day.

White Wolves

Teachers' Resource for Guided Reading Year 3

Stories with familiar settings

© A & C Black 2004

Detective Dan: Lesson 4

Summary of Chapter Four

On Friday Dan feels miserable as he goes to school. Not even the fact that he has an extra big sardine sandwich and that Minnie likes him again cheers him up! Dan's lunch box is once again knocked off the shelf. The food is all over the floor but the sandwich has gone.

Lesson plan

Introduction

Go around the group asking the children for one sentence at a time to summarise the story so far. Help the children to make the point briefly and clearly.

Reading

Read the chapter out loud in the group, concentrating at first on accurate reading and expression.

1) If necessary, demonstrate how to read sentences in order to show the sense.

2) Focus on any words the children have difficulties with and discuss ways to read them. In particular, "biscuit" (p. 35) and "anywhere" (p. 36) – another compound word to recognise.

Understanding the story

Ask the children some of these questions to check their understanding. Questions could be asked during reading or at the end of the chapter. Encourage the children to find the appropriate part in the text and not to try to rely on memory.

1) Why was Dan so unhappy when he went to school on Friday? What happened that *might* have cheered him up? Why do the children think this didn't help? (Minnie did not cheer him up as usual because he had been blamed for letting her into school earlier in the week.)

2) Why didn't Dan want to share Billy's sandwiches? Can the children infer that Dan is so miserable he doesn't want to eat?

Discussion

Open a discussion about the children's favourite lunch box snacks. Do they always eat the same things at dinnertime? If they have school dinners they could talk about what they would like to have in their lunch box. How would they feel if what happened to Dan had happened to them?

What to do next: The children can now complete Activity Sheet 4: "Dan's lunch on Friday" which is about the contents of a lunch box.

Dan's lunch on Friday

1. Dan's Mum has just made his lunch on Friday. She is going to put it into the box so he can take it to school. Draw what he takes inside the box. Label each item.

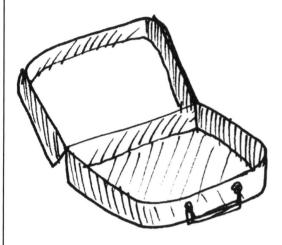

2. Now draw what you would like to eat at lunchtime. Label each item.

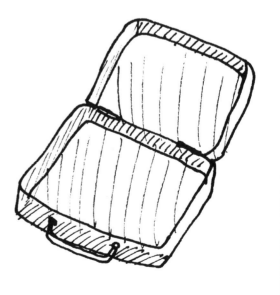

Summary of Chapter Five

After lunch Mrs Harper talks to the class about what has been happening and finds out that Dan is the only one who likes sardine sandwiches. Suddenly, Dan realises what has been happening and explains it to the class. They look into the cloakroom and, sure enough, Minnie is on the shelf sniffing at Dan's box. Mrs Harper says that Dan has done a good job as a detective. The boys are much happier as they run home at the end of the week.

Lesson plan

Introduction

Ask the children to talk about the clues in the story which explain what has been happening to Dan's lunch so far.

Reading

Read the chapter out loud in the group, concentrating at first on accurate reading and expression.

1) If necessary, demonstrate how to read sentences in order to show the sense.

2) Focus on any words the children have difficulties with and discuss ways to read them, in particular: "anyone" (p. 37) which is another compound word; "listening" (p. 39) with its silent "t"; "through" (p. 39); and "thought" and "though" (p. 41) – the similarities between these words may cause confusion.

Understanding the story through drama

Ask one of the children to play the part of Dan and put him in the hot seat. He starts to tell the others what has been going on during the week. The rest of the group and the teacher ask questions about what happened, why it happened and how Dan felt. Look back at the pictures in the book as stimulus for what to talk about.

What to do next: The children can now complete Activity sheet 5: "Minnie, the school cat" which is about what Minnie did during the week. Encourage the children to write something different for each day.

Minnie, the school cat

Day	Did Minnie like Dan?	What happened to the lunchbox?
Monday		
Tuesday		
Wednesday		
Thursday		
Friday		

Buffalo Bert by Michaela Morgan

About the book

Sunny thinks her unconventional "cowboy" grandfather, Bert, is great – until she starts at a new school, and worries that her new friends won't be impressed. She tries to find Bert new, normal hobbies suitable for someone his age. In the end, she confesses her feelings and Bert is upset. When Sunny's friends come round, he agrees to make himself scarce. However, it's impossible for Bert to keep quiet for long and, to Sunny's surprise, his antics delight her new friends.

There, framed and on display were:
A picture of me as a baby wearing only a sunhat and a huge toothless grin.

A picture of me in a paddling pool wearing only orange blow-up armbands.

A picture of me running round in a nappy and carrying a toy ducky.

30

Three terrible pictures perched on the window sill!
Binni, Kirsty and Nick hadn't spotted them yet, so I pushed my three friends on to the sofa, jumped past them, grabbed the pictures and shoved them behind the curtains quickly.

31

I used to think my Gramps was fantastic!
He used to tell me cowboy bedtime stories.

He used to sing me cowboy bedtime songs.

We used to have fun in the park.
I used to LOVE it!

8

But now I'm big I say: "Don't be silly, Gramps" or "Grow up, Gramps" and "Act your age!"

I bet *your* grandad doesn't wear a cowboy belt, a cowboy shirt and boots with spurs that jingle-jangle-jingle?

9

Buffalo Bert: Lesson 1

Summary of Chapter One

Sunny is not feeling very happy because of the way her Grandad behaves. He dresses and behaves like a cowboy! She used to like it when she was young – but not any more.

Lesson plan

Introduction

Try to find some pictures of buffaloes so that the children can refer to them when the word appears in the text. Explain that cowboys are men on horseback who round up cattle, especially in the Wild West of America.

Look at the front cover and read the blurb. What can the children tell about the character on the front cover? What do they think the story will be about?

Reading

Read the chapter out loud in the group, concentrating at first on accurate reading and expression.

1) If necessary, demonstrate how to read sentences in order to show the sense. For example, the slightly longer sentence at the bottom of p. 9.

2) Focus on any words the children have difficulties with and discuss ways to read them, for example: break up the word "buffalo" into syllables.

Understanding the story

Questions could be asked during reading or at the end of the chapter. Encourage the children to find the appropriate part in the text and not to try to rely on memory.

1) Why do the children think that Sunny used to think Gramps was fantastic?

2) Why do they think she has changed her mind? Look at the picture on p. 9 as a prompt to discussion.

3) Ask the children how they would feel? Do they think grandads should behave in a certain way? (This is covered in more detail in the second lesson.)

What to do next: The children can now complete Activity Sheet 1: "A Cowboy Grandad" which asks the children to answer some questions based on the chapter.

A Cowboy Grandad

Write around the picture all that you have found out about Buffalo Bert from reading Chapter One.

Buffalo Bert: Lesson 2

Summaries of Chapters Two and Three

Chapter Two: Sunny is embarrassed because Gramps is not like a "proper" grandad. She is worried because she has only been at her new school for three weeks and she wants to fit in with the other kids.

Chapter Three: Sunny wants to invite her three best friends to tea because she has been to their houses and had a really good time. However, she is worried that Gramps will embarrass her by dancing and singing and by wearing his cowboy clothes.

Lesson plan

Introduction
Ask the children to tell a partner what has happened so far.

Reading
Read the chapters out loud in the group, concentrating at first on accurate reading and expression. Stop at the end of chapter two to ask questions related to the text.

1) If necessary, demonstate how to read sentences in order to show the sense. For example: ensure that when the children read the second paragraph on p. 11, they pay attention to the comma so that the sentence flows.

2) Focus on any words the children have difficulties with and discuss ways to read them, for example: "probably", "guitar", "embarrassing".

Understanding the story
1) Ask the children what Sunny meant when she talked about a "proper grandad". How did she know what a proper grandad is? Discuss what Sunny thought on p. 11 and then ask the children if they agree. Do they think all grandads are the same? If they haven't already done so, they may like to talk about things their own grandads do.

2) Ask one of the children to play the part of Sunny in the hot seat.

The others ask questions about what she is worrying about and why, for example:

- Why don't you think your Gramps is a proper grandad?
- What is a proper grandad like?
- How is Bert different?
- Why are you so embarrassed by him?
- What do you think will happen when your friends come to tea?

The questioners should listen carefully to the answers and try to ask questions that lead on from what is said. For example Sunny might be asked "Why are you so embarrassed by your grandad?". If the reply is "I don't like some of the things he does" the obvious next step is to ensure that another question finds out what "things" refers to. If the next questioner asks an unrelated question, the teacher could intervene to explain how to question and answer carefully.

Can the children infer after the questioning what Sunny is bothered about – that she thinks Gramps should behave more like her expectation of a grown-up. Why do they think he behaves like this? They may mention that he likes cowboy stories or that he likes dressing up or that he is a cheerful person. Ask the children to discuss whether they would like to meet a cowboy grandad.

3) Ask the children what Sunny thinks will happen after her friends have come to tea. Can they deduce that she thinks they might not be friends with her once they meet her grandad?

4) Sunny was embarrassed by Gramps. Ask the children if they have ever felt embarrassed by something that has happened to them.

What to do next: The children can now complete Activity Sheet 2: "Oh dear, I'm so worried" which is about Sunny's thoughts and worries.

"Oh, dear. I'm so worried!"

What is Sunny worried about? Use the pictures to help you.

Buffalo Bert: Lesson 3

Summary of Chapter Four

Sunny tries to interest Gramps in new hobbies but he doesn't like anything she suggests. In the end she tells him the truth and admits that she doesn't want him in the house when her friends come. Gramps tells her that he will stay out of the way in the garden when her friends come. Although she is sorry that she has made Gramps sad, Sunny is glad that everything is sorted out because she wants the visit to be perfect.

Lesson plan

Introduction
Use the work done on Activity Sheet 3 to remind the children what Sunny was worried about.

Reading
Read Chapter Four out loud in the group, concentrating at first on accurate reading and expression.

1) If necessary demonstrate how to read sentences in order to show the sense. For example: ensure that the children can read the long sentence at the top of p. 19 without pausing in the wrong places.

2) Focus on any words the children have difficulties with and discuss ways to read them, for example: suggested, pensioners ("sh" sound in the middle of the word) and different.

Demonstrate how to break these up into syllables in order to read them correctly.

Understanding the story
1) Ask the children why Sunny pointed out all the clubs. Do they understand that she is trying to turn him into "proper grandad" and give him something to do to keep him out of the house.

2) Ask the children to imagine that they are Gramps. Why didn't he like the ideas? Can they deduce that many of those things are associated with growing old? What do they think Gramps feels about growing old?

3) Ask the children if they found anything funny in this chapter. They may mention the list of plans or the clubs themselves. This will depend upon the sense of humour of the children in the group and how much they understand Sunny's dilemma.

4) Ask the children how Gramps's behaviour changed after Sunny told him the truth. What do they think about the fact that she asked him to stay away from her friends. Open this up to general discussion. Was she right?

What to do next: The children can now complete Activity Sheet 3: "Thinking out loud" which is about what Gramps might have said to Sunny.

Thinking out loud

What Sunny said

"There are millions of clubs you can join."

"What about going to the Old Age Pensioners' Tea Party?"

"Well why not go to this talk called Looking after your toenails?"

"Are you OK, Gramps?"

What Gramps wanted to say

"

"

"

"

Buffalo Bert: Lesson 4

Summary of the first half of Chapter Five

Sunny's friends come round. Things do not go well at first when they find out that there is no DVD or computer. Mum tells them there will be sausage, chips and beans – and a special surprise. Suddenly, Sunny spots three photos of herself as a baby and she hides them quickly. But she also notices that Gramps is in the garden. He is wearing his cowboy clothes and is singing to himself. She draws the curtains so her friends don't see him and switches on the television. However, there is nothing good on any channel and Sunny's house does not have digital or satellite. Kirsty suggests that they go into the garden but, of course, Sunny will not let them do that. They all slump on the sofa, looking bored.

Lesson plan

Introduction
Ask the children to tell the story so far as briefly as possible.

Reading
Read the first half of the chapter out loud in the group, concentrating at first on accurate reading and expression.

If necessary, demonstrate how to read sentences in order to show the sense, for example:

- Demonstrate how to read the first sentence on p. 29 with a slight pause after the "and". Ask the children why they think it was written like that. Can they suggest that Mum was trying to make the dinner sound more exciting?

- Make sure they can read the long sentence on p. 31 so that the pace is clear.

- Focus on any words the children have difficulties with and discuss ways to read them, for example:

- Photographs ("f" sound) – can the children suggest any other words that start with "ph" and are pronounced "f"?

- Surprised (p. 34).

- Interesting (p. 34).

- Special ("sh" sound) (p.34).

- Digital (p. 35).

Understanding the story

1) Ask the children if they think Sunny is having a nice time so far when her friends come to tea. Encourage them to find all the evidence in the first part of the chapter:

- feeling embarrassed about not having a DVD or computer (pp. 27-28).
- spotting the photographs (p. 30).
- seeing Gramps out in the garden (p. 32).
- finding there is nothing on the television (p. 34).
- feeling embarrassed about not having digital or satellite (p. 35).
- not being able to go into the garden because Gramps is out there (p. 36).

2) Sunny is very concerned about what her friends think. Do the children think she ought to be concerned? There is quite an advanced idea implied about being your own person but some Year Threes will be able to think about this. It would not be appropriate to ask children to discuss what they worry about in their own home when friends come round.

3) Ask the children to think about Gramps's feelings. Look again at p. 33.

- What is Gramps doing?
- How do they know?

Discuss the use of the speech bubbles. Ask the children when they have seen these before – they may start to discuss comics. Which words did the author leave out because of the speech bubbles? ("He sang").

Ask the children how the song makes them feel.

4) Look at the picture on p. 36. Ask each child in the group to take a part (Sunny, Binni, Nick and Kirsty) and say how they are feeling at that precise moment. What does the word "slumped" suggest about their mood. (They are bored.)

> **What to do next:** The children can now complete Activity Sheet 4: "What will happen next".

What will happen next?

Write what you think is going to happen next at Sunny's house.

We all slumped on the sofa and gazed at the telly. My friends looked at each other. Then they looked at me.

_____

_____

_____

_____

_____

_____

_____

_____

_____

_____

_____

_____

Buffalo Bert: Lesson 5

Summary of the end of Chapter Five

Suddenly, Kirsty hears Gramps's singing (because it is getting louder). Sunny says it is only chickens. Then they hear a guitar and smell burning. Before Sunny can stop them, her friends pull the curtains and see Gramps. They assume that the surprise Sunny's mum mentioned is a campfire tea and they think Sunny is really lucky to have such a cool cowboy grandad. Sunny's friends have a great time and they want to come again! They end the day by singing round the campfire.

Lesson plan

Introduction
Share the different predictions that the children have written on their copies of Activity Sheet 4.

Reading
Read the end of the chapter out loud in the group, concentrating at first on accurate reading and expression.

1) If necessary demonstrate how to read sentences in order to show the sense. For example:

- Demonstrate reading the last sentence on p. 37 in order to show the stutter and an emphasis on the word "did".

- p. 38: "NO ... go to bed." Can the children read this to show that Sunny doesn't know what to say and is making it up as she goes along!

2) Focus on any words the children have difficulties with and discuss ways to read them. For example:

- Yodelling (make sure that the children understand that a yodel is a type of call in which the voice alternates between a normal pitch and a very high one) (p. 37).

- Stammered (p. 37).

- Strumming (p.39).

- "Yippeeeay ay and yodellayyaaa" (use phonics knowledge to read accurately) (p.42).

Understanding the story

1) Ask the children why Sunny made up the stories about the chicken and the radio?

2) Read aloud the words of the song. Make sure the rhymes are clear.

Now look at the top of p. 43. "I looked at my friends. What were they going to say?" Ask the children what Sunny thought they would say.

3) Look at p. 43. "Oh I see ... the surprise is we're having a campfire tea!" Ask the children when a surprise was mentioned before. (p. 29)

4) Ask the children if they found anything funny in chapter five. Remind them of what they read last lesson. They may talk about the photographs and about Sunny trying to suggest that the singing was a chicken!

Another rhyme – optional activity
Use the rhyme on p. 46 and work together to make another verse out loud – from the point of view of Sunny or her friends. An example could be:

We'll sing out loud and we'll sing all night
Because Sunny's grandad is more than all right
He dances, he raps, he yodels and much more
He's a wild cowboy grandad and never a bore.

> **What to do next:** The children can now complete Activity Sheet 5: "Hey, Mum! Guess what?" which is about what Sunny's friends might say when they got home that day.

"Hey, Mum! Guess what!"

Write what you think Binni, Nick and Kirsty said to their mums when they got home. Use the pictures to remind you what happened.

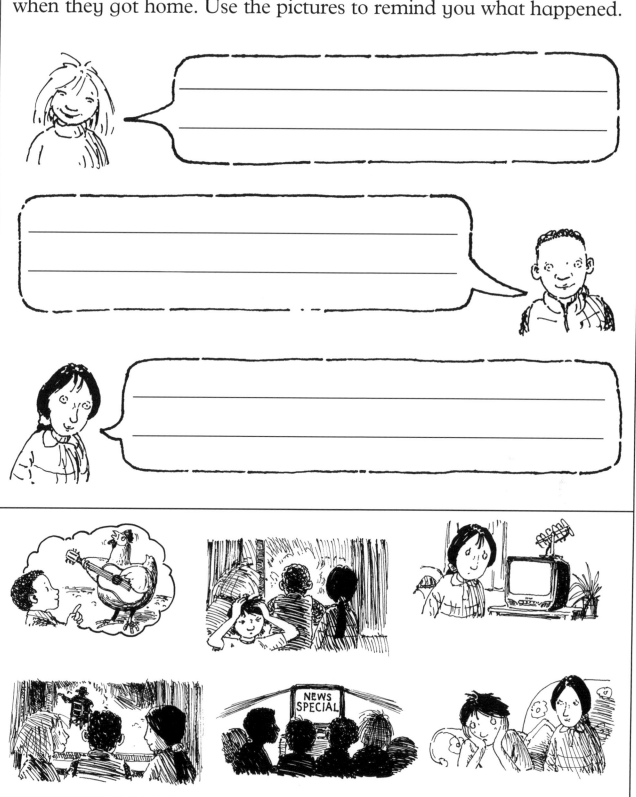

White Wolves

Teachers' Resource for Guided Reading Year 3

Stories with familiar settings

© A & C Black 2004

Treasure at the Boot-fair by Chris Powling

Cal's mum has arranged for him to help out old Mr Jessop on his bric-a-brac stall at the boot-fair on Saturday morning. He's too young to be paid; Cal is working to learn some responsibility. It's a quiet morning, but everything changes when Cal is left on his own. A young girl comes by, desperate to sell him a watch for only £10. After she's gone, Cal discovers the watch is worth a hundred times that. He knows it's only fair to tell the girl, and sets off after her. She is difficult to catch and reluctant to hand over the watch. In the end, Cal returns empty-handed to Mr Jessop. He is embarrassed, but it turns out he made the right decision. The girl was Mr Jessop's grand-daughter and both had planned the incident as a test of Cal's strength of character.

The old man looked happy enough, though. He tilted his umbrella and peered hopefully at the sky. "Know anything about bric-a-brac, Cal?" he asked.

"Bric-a-brac?"

"Antiques, son – except not so posh."

8

Mr Jessop pointed at the fold-up table in front of him. The top of it was divided into boxes – dozens of boxes. Each box was cluttered with oddments. Cal glanced at them and pulled a face. "Looks like a lot of junk to me," he said.

"That's because you haven't read *The Handbook*."

"The handbook?" asked Cal.

9

Treasure at the Boot-fair: Lesson 1

Summary of Chapter One

One rainy Saturday, Cal is going to help sell bric-a-brac at the boot-fair. The owner of the stall, Mr. Jessop, shows him the bric-a-brac handbook and tells him that it is like a map that leads to hidden treasure. He says that it is important to play fair with people. Cal is not in a good mood and does not want to be spending the day helping Mr Jessop.

Lesson plan

Introduction to the book

Look at the front cover and read the blurb. Ask the children:

- Where will this story be set?
- What is a boot-fair? Some children will be more familiar with the term "car boot sale".
- What does the word "treasure" suggest?
- What do the children think the story will be about?

Reading and comprehension

Read the chapter out loud in the group, concentrating at first on accurate reading and expression. Encourage the children to show the feelings of the two characters by the way the sentences are read.

1) If necessary, demonstrate how to read sentences in order to show the sense.

2) Focus on any words the children have difficulties with and discuss ways to read them.

3) Look at "weird as a widget". A widget is a gadget but Mr Jessop is not comparing himself to a gadget. Why does he use this expression? What is his meaning? (The children might see that it is the alliteration that is most important and the expression has been chosen to highlight the fact that Mr Jessop knows he's a bit odd!)

4) What is bric-a-brac? Ask the children to read pp. 9-10 again. They should realise that bric-a-brac has been described as "oddments" before the phrase is used.

Understanding the story

Questions could be asked during reading or at the end of the chapter. Encourage the children to find the appropriate part in the text and not to try to rely on memory.

1) Why isn't Cal happy? Encourage the children to find reasons from different parts of the chapter.

2) Why do the children think Cal said, "Not really" on p. 7 when he didn't mean it? (Notice the word "fibbed". He doesn't want to seem rude to Mr Jessop.)

3) Why did Mr. Jessop peer "hopefully" at the sky on p. 8. What does it tell the children? (He is an optimist and tries to see the best in things – he hopes the bad weather will clear.)

4) What do the children think "The Handbook" is all about? Focus on the word "treasure". Do they think Mr. Jessop means real treasure?

5) Why does Mr. Jessop tap his nose? What is he saying by doing this? (He is suggesting an element of secrecy.)

6) Do the children think Cal understands what Mr. Jessop means by playing fair with people? What is their evidence? They should notice the use of the word "shrugged". It suggests that he isn't really interested and he probably hasn't thought about it enough to know if he understands or not!

> **What to do next:** The children can now complete Activity Sheet 1: "The characters" which focuses on what the reader knows about Mr Jessop and Cal.

The characters

Write what you know about Cal and Mr. Jessop around the pictures. You can write about their thoughts and how they look.

White Wolves

Teachers' Resource for Guided Reading Year 3

Stories with familiar settings

© **A & C Black 2004**

Summary of Chapter Two

Cal is left to look after the stall for a while. A girl arrives with a Rolex watch belonging to her grandfather. She seems upset. He wonders if the watch is "hidden treasure" and agrees to buy it. He gives the girl £10 but thinks he hears her giggling as she hurries away.

Lesson plan

Introduction

Ask the children to summarise what has happened so far in two or three sentences.

Reading and comprehension

Read the chapter out loud in the group, concentrating at first on accurate reading and expression.

1) If necessary, demonstrate how to read sentences in order to show the sense.

2) Focus on any words the children have difficulties with and discuss ways to read them. For example: "definitely" (p. 20).

3) Ensure the children understand the meanings of the following words and expressions. Encourage them to read around the word to work it out:

- "hold the fort" (p. 13).
- "Jimmy Riddle" (p. 13) (cockney rhyming slang).
- "skimpy" (pp. 15-16). Use picture clues to help.

Understanding the story

Questions could be asked during reading or at the end of the chapter. Encourage the children to find the appropriate part in the text and not to try to rely on memory. Some of these points appear on the activity sheet so teachers can decide whether they want to discuss them in advance or not.

1) Why did the girl want to sell the watch?

2) Why didn't Cal want to buy it at first?

3) What do the children think changed his mind? (They should discuss a number of points: he is affected because the girl is upset; he wonders if it is hidden treasure.)

4) Does Cal think he has done the right thing? The children should notice the fact that he crosses his fingers – he hopes it is right but he isn't sure.

5) Why does the girl's mood change on p. 21?

6) What do the children think Cal must have thought when he heard her giggling?

> **What to do next:** The children can now complete Activity Sheet Two: "The watch" which focuses on what has happened in Chapter Two.

The watch

Answer these questions about the events in Chapter Two.

1) Why did the girl want to sell the watch?

_____

_____

_____

2) Why didn't Cal want to buy it at first?

_____

_____

_____

3) Why do you think Cal changed his mind?

_____

_____

_____

4) Do you think the girl really was upset? Explain your answer carefully.

_____

_____

_____

5) What do you think is going to happen next?

_____

_____

Summary of Chapter Three

Cal believes that he has been tricked and realises that he should have checked in the handbook before buying the watch. He looks at it and, to his amazement, discovers that it is very valuable. At first he thinks that Mr. Jessop will be pleased because he has made a huge profit. However, he remembers what the old man said about playing fair.

Lesson plan

Introduction

Ask the children to tell a partner in one minute what has happened so far. Ask each child to make one quick point about what they think will happen next.

Reading and comprehension

Read the chapter out loud in the group, concentrating at first on accurate reading and expression.

1) If necessary, demonstrate how to read sentences in order to show the meaning.

2) Focus on any words the children have difficulties with and discuss ways to read them. In particular ask one of the children to re-read the description of the watch on p. 24. Explain:

- Rolex is a brand of expensive watches – it would be a good idea to have some colour pictures available.
- Oyster – the range (like a Fiesta is a type of Ford).
- Bubble back – the back of the watch is a domed shape.
- Perpetual – is wound up by the movement of the wrist.
- Automatic – doesn't need winding by hand.
- Blue sweep second hand – a large second hand, blue in colour.
- c – short for "circa" – Latin for "about".

3) "As if to torment him …" (p. 22) What does "torment" mean? (It means causing physical or mental suffering.)

4) What does "double-checked the details" mean on p. 25? (It means looking twice at something to ensure your first impressions were correct.)

5) Ensure that the children understand what "profit" (p. 26) means. (Profit is the amount of money left when the cost of something is deducted from the price it was sold at.)

Understanding the story

Ask one of the children to play the part of Cal and sit in the hot seat. Ask the other children to question him to find out how he was feeling at different points in the chapter. If necessary, prompt with some questions to find out:

- why Cal thinks he has been tricked
- what his first reaction was when he read what the watch was worth
- what he thought when he remembered what Mr. Jessop had said about playing fair.

What to do next: The children can now complete Activity Sheet 3: "The bric-a-brac handbook" which focuses on describing another watch.

The Bric-A-Brac handbook

Draw a picture of your own watch – or one belonging to a friend or member of your family.

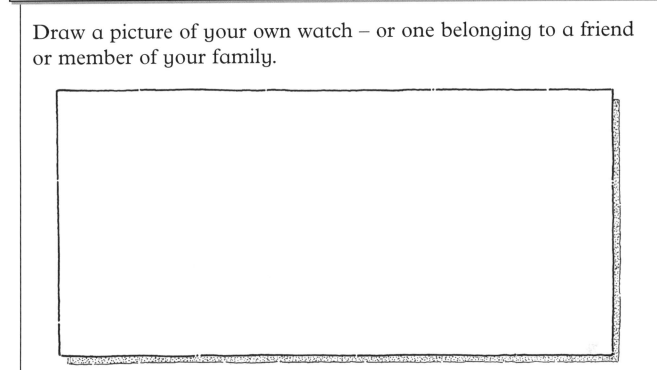

Write a short piece of information about the watch that might be in the bric-a-brac handbook. Try to write it in "notes" like the Rolex entry in the story.

Treasure at the Boot-fair: Lesson 4

Summary of Chapter Four

Cal decides to pack all the bric-a-brac up and take it with him to follow the girl. She has been seen heading for the bus stop. He catches up with her as she is boarding the bus. The girl immediately says that he can't have his money back but he tells her that the watch is really valuable. She takes the watch from him and is examining it as the bus pulls away.

Lesson plan

Introduction

Quickly re-tell the story so far by asking each child to add a sentence in turn.

Reading and comprehension

Read the chapter out loud in the group, concentrating at first on accurate reading and expression.

1) If necessary, demonstrate how to read sentences in order to show the meaning.

2) Focus on any words the children have difficulties with and discuss ways to read them. In particular check pronunciation of: "especially" (p. 29); "quickened" (p. 30); "wary" (p. 32); "valuable" (p. 33).

3) What does "Looked like a puff of wind would blow her away" tell the reader about the appearance of the girl? What word has already been used to describe her? (Skimpy). Again use pictures to support the discussion.

4) Discuss with the children the meanings of "wary" (p. 32 – means hesitant or cautious) and "impressed" (p. 34 – means to make you feel in admiration of someone or something) and what the words tell the reader about the reaction of the girl at that point. It seems that the girl is rather nervous about Cal's approach and what he is telling her.

Understanding the story – drama

Put the children in pairs – one taking the part of Cal and the other of the girl. Ask them to role play the incident by the bus stop. "Cal" must explain why he has followed her. "The girl" must show her changing reaction.

> **What to do next:** The children can now complete Activity Sheet 4: "How do they feel?" which focuses on the changing feelings of the characters in this chapter. The children should read to the end of the book before the next lesson.

How do they feel?

Write down how Cal and the girl feel at different points in Chapter Four and why.

1. When Cal first decides to follow the girl,
he feels _____

_____

_____

_____

2. As Cal follows her up the lane towards the bus stop,
he feels _____

_____

_____

_____

3. When the girl first spots Cal, she feels

_____

_____

_____

_____

4. When Cal tells the girl that the watch is valuable,
she feels _____

_____

_____

_____

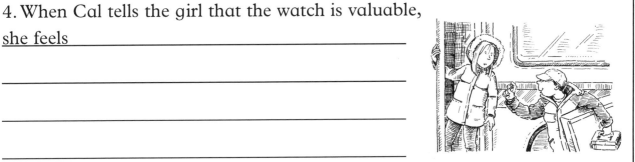

Summary of Chapter Five

Mr Jessop is waiting for Cal when he returns. He is no longer cheerful and friendly. Cal tells him what has happened. He is surprised to find that the old man seemed to be laughing by the time he had finished the story. Cal suddenly realises that he had been set up. Mr Jessop explains that the girl is his grand-daughter and she checks out the new helpers. He asks Cal to help him permanently and the boy agrees.

Lesson plan

Introduction
Ask the children to explain what happened in the chapter that they read independently.

Reading and comprehension
1) Ask some of the children to re-read certain sentences in order to check pronunciation. For example:
• "awkwardly" (p. 37).
• "ignition" (p. 38.)

2) Ask the children which words and phrases on pp. 35 and 36 tell us that Mr Jessop was not pleased. ("coldly", "wobbled dangerously", "... didn't seem quite so smiley now").

3) Ask the children the meaning of these words and expressions:
• "put your brain in gear" (p. 40) – to think seriously and carefully about something.
• "a set-up" (p. 42) – a situation which is created to trick or catch someone out).
• "a wally" (p. 43) – a silly person.
• "permanent" (p. 44) – lasting.

Understanding the story through drama
Give all the children a role – Cal, Mr Jessop or the girl. It does not matter if more than one child has the same part.

The children should stay in role and talk about:
• the plan – why Mr. Jessop did it; how the girl felt when she was carrying it out;
• how they feel at the end of the story.

> **What to do next:** The children can now complete Activity Sheet 5: "What do you think?" which focuses on the whole story.

What do you think?

Answer these questions about "Treasure at the Boot-fair".

1. What do you think Cal might have said if you asked him if he had a good day?

_____

_____

_____

_____

_____

2. Mr. Jessop's grand-daughter was an actress. Why did he ask her to join in his plan? How could an actress help?

_____

_____

_____

_____

3. Do you think Mr. Jessop did the right thing?

_____

_____

_____

_____

White Wolves

Teachers' Resource for Guided Reading Year 3

Stories with familiar settings

© A & C Black 2004

Record Card

Group:	Book:
Focus for session:	

Names	Comments

About the Author: Vivian French

Vivian French

Vivian French once said that she has always been addicted to words. One of her first jobs was as an actor in a theatre company, but she decided it would be more fun to share stories, so she became a storyteller. Eventually, she started writing her stories down and her first books were published in 1990. When she writes a book now, she acts it out in her head and always knows how the characters sound and move. She has written over two hundred books and is always in demand to tell stories in schools and at conferences.

The White Wolves Interview

Where did the idea for Detective Dan come from?
The idea for Dan came from real life – one of my daughters took sardine sandwiches to school and the school cat just wouldn't leave her alone!

What's the hardest thing about writing stories – and the easiest?
The hardest thing about writing stories is finishing them! Beginnings are fine, and middles aren't *too* bad, but finding a good ending is Very Hard Work. The easiest thing (and the nicest) about writing stories is talking to the lovely editors.

What do you enjoy doing when you're not writing?
If I'm not writing (and I don't always enjoy writing) I love chatting to friends, pottering about Edinburgh (where I live), and listening to music – especially live music.

What did you enjoy reading when you were young – and what do you enjoy reading now?
When I was young I read everything I could get my hands on (even the back of the cornflakes packet). My dad went to the library every week and brought us back books; I didn't really mind what he chose, but I did love *The Box of Delights* by John Masefield. At the moment I'm reading a book about a famous diary writer called Samuel Pepys and it's *fascinating* ... I love reading about other people's lives. (I think it's because I'm nosey!)

Michaela Morgan

Michaela has written over one hundred books for children, including junior fiction, picture books, poetry and non-fiction. She often visits schools to talk about her books and to encourage children with their own writing. Michaela says, "I get my inspiration by being a nosey parker. I listen to what people are saying. I look at what they are doing. Then I let my imagination take over." Michaela spends some of her time in Hove in Sussex and some of her time in rural France and enjoys travelling.

The White Wolves Interview

Where did the idea for Buffalo Bert come from?
I saw a man walking around town, dressed like a cowboy. I started to wonder about him …

What's the hardest thing about writing stories – and the easiest?
For me the easiest thing is getting the idea and writing the first draft. The hardest thing is working on the story to revise and improve it.

What do you enjoy doing when you're not writing?
Lying around and daydreaming.

What did you enjoy reading when you were young – and what do you enjoy reading now?
I liked Roald Dahl's *The BFG* and Lewis Carroll's *Alice in Wonderland* and Enid Blyton's *The Famous Five* and … loads of things.

Chris Powling

Chris Powling was born in South London, where he still lives with his wife, Jan. He spent twenty years as a teacher in London schools and ten years as a lecturer in children's literature. In fact, just about everything that Chris has ever done has been connected to books and writing. He has judged literary awards, spent seven years as the editor of the children's books magazine Books for Keeps, and now reviews books on radio.

The White Wolves Interview

Where did the idea for Treasure at the Boot-fair come from?
From a boot-fair, where else! A couple of friends of mine (to whom the book is dedicated) came across a Rolex watch on a stall at a local boot-fair. The stall-holder wasn't the least bit interested. Later, after Sheila and David got the Rolex cleaned and repaired, they discovered its real value. When they told me the story, I started thinking ... and Cal, his mum and the mysterious Mr

Jessop slowly took shape in my mind.

What's the hardest – and the easiest – thing about writing stories?
For me, the dialogue is the easiest. Once I've got a clear idea of my characters, their voices seem to chatter away in my head. The main problem is making sure they don't talk *too* much! The hardest thing is pacing the story – making sure it doesn't move too quickly, too slowly or too predictably. Reading it aloud as I write is probably the best help with this.

What do you enjoy doing when you're not writing?
I read, read, read ... all writers do, I think. Normally, I've got at least three different books on the go at one time. When I'm not reading, I'll probably be watching Charlton Athletic, my local football club. I've supported the team for more than fifty years now and am far too old to stop.

What did you enjoy reading when you were young – and what do you enjoy reading now?
As a youngster, I read any book I could get my hands on – usually from my local library (to which I still belong). Fiction, non-fiction, picture books – I loved them all. Nowadays, nothing much has changed. Actually, because I talk about books each month on radio (Classic FM), I'm even *paid* to read lots and lots of books. Can you imagine how lucky I feel?

Year 3

Dan is in trouble at school, but he isn't to blame. If he and Billy become detectives, can they solve the mystery together?

There's been a robbery at Doogood's furniture shop but Police Constable Penny Penrose has been ordered to count traffic cones. Still, that doesn't stop her dogs, Scratch and Sniff getting on the case. Apart from sticky buns, there's nothing they like better than a good mystery to solve...

Buffalo Bert isn't like any other grandad. He's always doing crazy things. Sunny thinks Bert is great – until she makes a new set of friends at school.

As Scott passes the basement steps of his new school, there's a bang and a crash and a roaring sound. Scott knows there's something down there... something nasty... something dangerous. What is it? Can Scott piece together the clues and solve the mystery?

Cal is helping out on Mr Jessop's stall. It's a tough job. He needs to be quick, clever and fair – especially when something valuable comes along.

There are signs of a ghost in Granpa's creaky old house. Bits of it have been left in the chimney and you can hear its heartbeat at night. So when Adam dares his brother and sister to get on the ghost trail and hunt it down in the graveyard at midnight, who will be brave enough to go with him?

This resource will help teachers use three White Wolves books for guided reading lessons in the classroom. It includes five guided reading teaching sequences plus photocopiable worksheets for each of the books.

This resource will help teachers use three White Wolves books for guided reading lessons in the classroom. It includes five guided reading teaching sequences plus photocopiable worksheets for each of the books.

White Wolves Resources for Guided Reading

Year 4

When Hugo breaks his arm, he thinks he'll be bored and useless. But with his mum's new reaching, grabbing and twirling invention, Hugo's world is turned upside down!

Luke loves visiting his grandad and helping out with the pigeons. But Grandad gets sick and muddled and needs more than Luke's help. When he goes into hospital, events take a turn for the worst and suddenly Luke has to grow up very fast...

Zoey leads an ordinary life, but her secret wishes are far from normal. One magical day, she logs on to the net and finds she has the chance to make her wildest dreams come true.

Carly is being teased and excluded from the group of girls who were once her best friends. She tries to put a brave face on it, but it's clear that she has "lost her fizz". Then Carly finds a stray dog that needs a loving home and all at once life starts looking very different...

How did Caleb turn into a creature part boy and part swan, and come to live on the Isle of Nanna? Find out in this haunting story from a prize-winning writer.

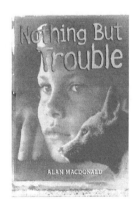

It's a tough job being Jago's "buddy" at school. The new boy comes from a family of travellers and he doesn't say much or seem interested in making friends. Then Paul discovers Jago has a secret and a special bond develops between the two boys, but how long can it last?

This resource will help teachers use three White Wolves books for guided reading lessons in the classroom. It includes five guided reading teaching sequences plus photocopiable worksheets for each of the books.

This resource will help teachers use three White Wolves books for guided reading lessons in the classroom. It includes five guided reading teaching sequences plus photocopiable worksheets for each of the books.

White Wolves Resources for Guided Reading

.... Year 5 .... Year 6 ....

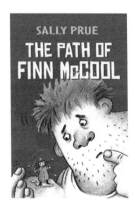

When the giant Finn McCool annoys the little people, they warn him of an even bigger giant across the sea in Scotland. Finn's big mistake is setting off to find him...

Margaret Mahy is renowned for creating vivid fantasy landscapes that enthral readers of all ages. This collection brings together five Mahy classics – by turns madcap, haunting and surreal.

Many years ago, there lived a lazy barber who lost customers by cutting them, not their hair! Luckily, he had a clever wife with cunning plans to earn the couple money...

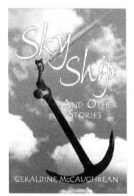

Geraldine McCaughrean has won many awards for stories set in the past. Here are five brilliant tales that will transport you to other times and places you will never forget.

A boy drinks from the magic cauldron of knowledge and is reborn as Taliesin. Now he has the power to change the fortunes of all whom he encounters – for better and for worse.

In Joan Aiken's stories, ghosts appear in both bizarre and familiar places – and none is easily forgotten. This collection of chillers is guaranteed to send a shiver down your spine.

This resource will help teachers use three White Wolves books for guided reading lessons in the classroom. It includes five guided reading teaching sequences plus photocopiable worksheets for each of the books.

This resource will help teachers use three White Wolves books for guided reading lessons in the classroom. It includes five guided reading teaching sequences plus photocopiable worksheets for each of the books.